Cajun Household Wisdom

CAJUN HOUSEHOLD WISDOM

"You Know You Still Alive If It's Costin' You Money!"

Collected, and with a Commentary, by

Kenneth Aguillard Atchity

LONGMEADOW
P R E S S

Copyright © 1995 by Kenneth Aguillard Atchity

Published by Longmeadow Press, 201 High Ridge Road, Stamford, CT 06904. All rights reserved. No part of this book may be reproduced or utilized in any form or by any means, electronic or mechanical, including photocopying, recording or by any information storage and retrieval system, without permission in writing from the Publisher. Longmeadow Press and the colophon are registered trademarks.

An AEI Book

Cover design by Kelvin Oden
Interior design by Richard Oriolo

Library of Congress Cataloging-in-Publication Data

Atchity, Kenneth John.
    Cajun household wisdom : you know you still alive, if it's costin' you money! / collected and with a commentary by Kenneth Aguillard Atchity. — 1st ed.
        p.   cm.
    ISBN 0-681-00772-9
    1. Proverbs, Cajun.   I. Title.
PN6455.L8A83   1994
398.9'41—dc20   94-34558
                                             CIP

21,341

Printed in the United States of America

First Edition

0 9 8 7 6 5 4 3 2 1

For Myrza Marie Aguillard Atchity
and in loving memory of
Mezille Latiolais Aguillard ("Mémère")

Photo by Russell Lee

"**H**ighway Directions"

PREFACE

This is an unabashedly eccentric collection, more remembered than researched: comments and malapropisms heard after the guests departed in my partly diaspora, partly rooted French Louisiana maternal family. When I grew up, as a half-time resident eating my way from Baton Rouge to Breaux Bridge to Maringouin to Grand Isle to Breaux Bridge to Eunice to Iota to Lake Charles to Basile to Melville, much of the wisdom I gleaned came from the kitchen where most of the eating also took place—much of it standing guard over the Magnalite pots. But the bedroom isn't a bad source either (where we're awakened every morning with a tray of coffee); or the front porch, where we rock and talk; or the back porch where we clean fish and shell field peas. Wherever, most of the best talking happens after the *cousins* who'd come over for dinner to see me had gone home.

Collected here are translations of sayings heard sometimes in Cajun French, sometimes in "Cajun English"—the last accounting for the idiomatic expressions like "ain't" and "nuttin'" for "sumptin'." The Cajuns, since they were told by law in 1929 that English was the official language of Louisiana, can speak standard English at gunpoint but are happier with their own idiomatic use of it. I've sometimes used the French spelling of French words, sometimes a phonetic English transcription so the reader can hear how the word is pronounced in South Louisiana (*sha*, for example, instead of *cher*). I've used Rev. Msgr. Jules O. Daigle's *Dictionary of the Cajun Language* when in doubt about a French Louisiana word. I've transcribed the Cajun English dialect as my ear remembers it, and not always consistently, because we have more than one way of saying a word. If that bothers you, I remind you of the story of the apocryphal Cajun who went up to Harvard to consider applying. He ran across a senior in Harvard Square.

Cajun: "Could you please tell me whar de administration office is at?"

Harvard senior: "Excuse me? I have no idea what you're saying. Don't you realize, young man, that it is improper to end a sentence with a preposition?"

Cajun: "Excuse *moi*. Could you tell me whar de administration office is at, *asshole*?"

I appreciate advice and help from Jeanne Louise Buillard, Dave Petitjean, Philip Gould, Susie Labry, Elemore Morgan, Jr., Chi-Li Wong and my Louisiana family: Buddy and Yvonne Aguillard, Robert Aguillard, Wilbur and Martha Aguillard, Ed and Willie Mae Aguillard, Carol Knight, and Hubert and Viola Martel.

Not too many of us applied to or got into Harvard, thank *le Bon Dieu*, though my friend from Breaux Bridge, Michael Rees, did—and he's talked funny ever since. So, as my cousin Hubert Martel would say, you make yo'self at home, heah?—if you doan, you be de loser!

KENNETH AGUILLARD ATCHITY
Los Angeles and Baton Rouge, May 1, 1994

Wake up an' smell de chickens.

No point in treein' dat coon if you ain't gonta shoot him.

Nevair git in a pissin' contess wid a skonk.

Det man lies so bad, his wife got ta call de hogs.

If his life's so bad, why ain't he dead yet?

It's hard to fool a Cajun. He knows that people love to complain—that complaining makes people happy.

He'd git lot moh done if he di'n't work so hard.

If he's so smart, how come he allays has sumptin' ta do?

You want ta communicate wid det man, you got ta stop talkin' ta him foh 'while.

Poo-yai! If you jes' shut up ah could heah you lot bedder.

No point in tellin' de trewt ta folks who bizy lyin' ta demselves.

De minute you start ta communicate wid dat fella, you in trouble.

How Dey Got Dis-A-Way

The French-speaking people of South Louisiana are generally referred to as Cajuns, a word corrupted from *Acadiens*, which in French means "Acadians"—after the province in Canada from which French-speaking Catholics were expelled by English-speaking Protestants in *le grand dérangement* between 1750 and 1770.

All Cajuns are Acadians, but not all Acadians are Cajuns. Acadians are all those descended from the inhabitants of Acadia, now known as Nova Scotia. Cajuns are those whose Acadian ancestors fled to Louisiana after the expulsion. They say the lobsters up there missed them so much, they followed afterward. By the time they reached Louisiana, the poor things had worn themselves down so much—they'd become crawfish.

But *nothing's* that simple in South Louisiana, either, where it's hard to find two people agreeing on anything except the need for food and music. Cajuns are distinguished from Creoles in South Louisiana (now known as "Acadiana," thanks to Paul Prudhomme and the Council for the Development of French in Louisiana, *CODOFIL*) differently than they are in New Orleans. In South Louisiana where I, my mother, and her parents were born, a Creole was a French-speaking, or French-descended, more or less Caucasian person who was *not* from Canada (this would include the Spanish, whose flag flew over the state for a while, but who learned to speak French when they had to). By that definition, the Aguillard family (my maternal grandfather's) as well as the Latiolais family (my maternal grandmother's) were Creole rather than Cajun. The Latiolais had been in Louisiana at least a half-century before the Cajuns arrived; the Aguilars came from Seville by way of the Canary Islands, supposedly in the employ of pirate-turned-war (of 1812) hero Jean Lafitte, about a half-century later. Like many of Spanish descent, upon seeing what a good thing the French had going in Louisiana, they changed their name from Aguilar to Aguillard.

But as close by as New Orleans (to its residents, Louisiana is informally divided into South Louisiana, North Louisiana— where *bayous* become *creeks*—and New Orleans), a Creole is a person of mixed blood, primarily from the Caribbean, and a

Cajun—well, a Cajun is a Caucasian who speaks French. So by New Orleans definition, the Aguillards *and* the Latiolais are Cajuns. Several of my direct ancestors, including a Broussard, a Thibodeaux, and a Patin, are listed in a log of arriving Acadians. If you haven't got at least one Thibodeaux in your family tree, you probably aren't from Louisiana at all. They may still argue about their origins, but the Cajuns and the Creoles have been cooking together in bed as well as in the kitchen for two hundred years.

Their culture, to this day, is characterized by the traits suggested throughout this little collection. It's funny. It's fun-loving (after all, the slogan of Acadiana today is *Laissez les bon temps roulez!*: "Let the good times roll!"). It's rooted in the earth. It's rooted in the kitchen. It's needlessly, nearly hopelessly, complicated with a sharp undertone of simplicity. It's initially cautious about outsiders but eternally loyal once it's let them in. It's suspicious of all things modern, especially when it comes to food and morals. Cajun culture believes that the best exercise, and the best therapy other than eating and laughing, is dancing—and in little towns throughout the state (in lounges like the Rainbeaux in New Iberia, the Green Frog in Lake Charles, Fred's in Mamou, the Purple Peacock in Eunice), you'll find people of all ages—from three to 103—dancing the two-step or the Cajun shuffle or the Cajun waltz at the *fais-do-do* nearly every night of the week). Being precocious among the Cajuns means you dance and drink coffee before you can walk.

Probably what impressed me most growing up with my aunts

and uncles (Bernice, whom I called Nan-ee because she was my godmother; Ruby; Wilbur; and Ed) was that they were all storytellers. The only thing they liked better than hearing a new story was telling an old one. And, of course, their stories evolved in the telling. My grandmother, Mezille, who died last year at the age of 97, couldn't read or write in French *or* in English. But she could sing ballads that lasted forty minutes, and she could tell you a story that lasted two hours. Her sister, Laurence (Lo-RONCE), couldn't read or write, either. But she kept track of phone numbers all right, by drawing a picture of turkeys next to my *grandmère*'s number (because Mezille's turkeys once pecked to death Evan's new '36 Chevrolet, parked for safety in the pasture), a picture of pigeons next to her daughter Kelsie Mae's. She had a pictorial directory to everyone in St. Landry Parish (there are no counties in Louisiana, the only state in the U.S. whose laws are still based on Napoleonic Code).

"The Oysterman"

Tell de trewt an' ruin de pardy.

You know you not at home if dey makin' you wear shoes.

You in big trouble w'en you have ta apologize foh bein' yo'self.

Ah tell you what—dey ain't no medicine kin cure stupidity.

You mix up your crazyness enough an' you be happy.

Dere is no way a man standin' on his two feet kin avoid trouble.

"Cajun Wedding"

Doan show up ta *mah* pardy 'less you plannin' ta dance.

De longest distance between two points is trew de dance hall.

You t'ink too much, you miss all de steps.

If at foist you doan succeed, go an' dance.

LEARNING
THE ROPES

All Cajun *grandmères* teach their grandchildren to play *bourré* (BOO-ray, which means "stuffed," because losers have to stuff the pot) and gin rummy as soon as they're old enough to say "gin," which my *grandmère* (we called her *"Mémère"*) always seemed to say first. To this day I have the feeling when I play gin that if you haven't knocked or ginned after the fourth card, you haven't learned how to play the game correctly. To begin with, you don't hold your cards in a fan. You hold them in a pyramid. It's ten times harder to hold them that way, but once you get the hang of it, you have a much wider view of the possibilities.

That's typical. Cajuns like to do *everything* in a way ten times harder than necessary. It's hard to explain this Cajun peculiarity, except by examples. My favorite example is the time my mother caught a twenty-pound catfish. Three times. First she hooked it, then reeled it toward the dock. She got a good look at the sucker before it broke her line. "He got my interest," she explained, to indicate why she dragged her picnic guests to the dock for the next six hours waiting for the fish to strike again. Next time she got it almost on the dock before it flopped away from her and broke her line again. Now there was no stopping her. She went inside and got a good night's sleep, but she was back at the dock early the next morning. Hours went by, then he struck again. She screamed for my sister Laurie to bring a net (typical of a Cajun that she *still* hadn't fore-armed herself with a net; the Cajun personality loves to tantalize fate, to see just how much will be required or how much can be gotten away with). Fortunately Laurie brought the net quickly and helped her land the fish. They got it on shore, and checked its mouth to prove my mother's point that it was the same fish. Indeed, all three of her lures were in its mouth! She got more joy out of that thrice-caught fish than out of the thousands and thousands she caught before or since (see photograph).

"Thrice-Caught Catfish"

Befoh you tame det gator, *sha*, be sure you kin keep feedin' him.

You doan know a man till you ate yo' way trew his house.

A man what doan know he's poor ain't poor, no.

Every man wears gloves foh his own reasons.

People don't wear gloves much in south Louisiana, for any
*reason—so this means just the opposite of what it might
mean in New England where you wear gloves to keep your
hands clean or warm. Here, it mean if a man wears gloves,
he's trying to keep you from seeing his hands, "He's up ta
no good," or, at the very least, "Ah wonder what he t'inks
he's doin' wearin' dose gloves, him."*

You take yo'self too seriously an' foh sure no
one else will.

You got ta git up oirly oirly ta keep de sun from rising.

Ah may not be raht, but ahm *sure*.

You doan got ta look too much below de surface if you got enough surface.

Some of the Cajuns became rice farmers. To grow a lot of rice you have to have a lot of land—I mean, many arpents *(36,864 square feet—the unit of land measure in Louisiana). This proverb has to do with the belief that if you own enough land, you don't need to have gold buried in it, or oil flowing under it. A lot of land in itself is good.*

Liqua' is de peephole on a man.

Ah tell you one t'ing—you better off dyin' of trink dan dyin' of thirst.

If you got ta have a reason, you doan got ta have de trink.

A HAPPY
DEATH

One day in Breaux Bridge, along the Bayou Teche, Hebert (ay-BEAR) told his friend Thibodaux (Tee-Boe-DOE) that he heard that Jax Brewery was hiring *en ville* (French for "downtown," referring to New Orleans) and that the two of them should make tracks there and clean up a fortune.

Thibodeaux said, "You know ah kin't do dat, man—ah just got married, me! My wife she would not unnerstand."

Hebert told Thibodeaux, "Leave her ta me," and went to see Mrs. Thibodeaux. "Lissen, *sha*," he told her, "you let me take yo' husban' *en ville* ta woik at dat brew'ry an' we gone be back befoh you know it, wid so much monaie yo' knees gonta shake."

Well, Mrs. T. allowed how that would be something, but said, "You take good care him, you heah?"

Two weeks later, Hebert rings her doorbell. Mrs. T. comes to the door, sees he's alone, and passes him some *bad* eyes.

"Whar's mah hosban'?"

"Ah got some bad news foh you, *sha*," Hebert says. "Yo' hosban' is daid."

"Doan tell me dat, anh?!" Mrs. T. says, threatening him with her fist.

"It's de trewt," Hebert says. "He done drownt hisself in a vat o' beer."

"No way!"

But Hebert nods. "He was sweeping around de vat, an' slip on some malt, an' he fall into de vat an' drownt!"

Mrs. T. is devastated. He has to hold her to keep her from fainting.

"Well, tell me," she finally asks, "did he suffer much?"

"No, ah doan believe so," Hebert says. "He got out t'ree times ta go ta de bat'room!"

"Lester Deville, Mamou"

If de gravy ain't no good, de jokes ain't gonta help.

If you kin't laugh, you kin't keep a friend.

He lost his mind, yah, but t'ank God he ain't lost his sense o' humor.

Folks what say all de fruit git ripe at de same time nevair had a strawberry patch.

Doan leave nuttin' de way you found it.

You got two choices: Fo'git yo' dreams—or pay foh dem.

Dere got ta be *sumptin'* ta him—'cause *nobody* laks him.

Ah doan dislike dat boy—ah just doan lak him around.

She t'inks her shit is sweet potata.

If you not fishin', you not doin' anyting serious.

De sleepin' man's net ketches de biggest fish.

"Redfish Catch"

Dat woman, she been makin' a *career* out o' constipation.

Blood is t'icker dan brains.

Money doan make you happier, *sha*—jes' make you crazier.

Folks what kin't afford it theyselves shouldn' spend udder folks's money.

You know you alive if it's costin' you money.

"The Men's Section at the *fais-do-do*"

You doan' need money once you on de dance floor.

In the old days you could attend a dance free, but you had to pay to be on the dance floor. Men with an eye to courting could make their choices from "the bull pen."

Somehow Cajuns don't seem to think a lot about money, except to poke fun at it. In all the years I've gone back to visit, I don't remember spending much time talking about finances. Cajuns are more interested in the texture of things than in the bottom line. I once heard someone say on a dance floor in Baton Rouge, "You kin git ta de bottom line as much as you want, *sha*, but you kin't *eat* it." That's why *Mémère* cut her food up in little tiny pieces. To make more texture. To make the taste last longer.

Most of the time is spent talking about eating, and the rest about how crazy people are in general: "Why does your mother fry her aigs like dat?" "Why does Willie Mae set her table after dinner?" When someone from somewhere else insists on talking about the economy, almost surely it will give rise to one of an infinite number of white horse parables (sometimes it's a white mule). Generally the storyteller gets so carried away he forgets the moral to the story, if there ever was one. Storytelling, like laughter, becomes an end in itself. Here's one of my favorites:

A man walks into a bar in Rain, Louisiana. He goes over to the bartender and asks, "Could you tell me, sah, who owns dat white mule dat's tied outside?"

The bartender nods toward the end of the bar, where another old farmer gestures with his bottle of Dixie and says, "Dat'd be me. Dat's mah mule, yah."

"Well, ah wanta tell you one ting," the other farmer says. "Dat's de finest mule ah've seen in a long time. Let me axe you, how much you would sole me dat mule foh?"

"Det mule's not for sale," the other man says. "Dat's mah favorite mule."

"Ah'll give you one hundert dollars foh him, cash, right now," says the first man.

"One hundert dollars? Cash?" the other man says. "Solt!"

The man hands over the money, and leaves with the mule. On the long walk home, the man who sold the mule says to himself, "Ah kin't believe ah sold det man mah white mule. Ah loved det mule. He was mah favorite mule. An' for sure dat man must know sumptin' 'bout him ta buy him foh a hundert dollars cash."

The next night the first man meets the second man in the same bar. "You know dat mule ah done solt you las' night?" he says.

"Yes, dat's one fine mule," the other man says.

"Ah'll give you two hundert dollars foh dat mule," the first man says. "Cash."

"Cash?" the other man says. "Solt!"

And he's walking home, thinking: "Ah kin't believe ah solt dat mule foh two hundert dollars when last night ah wanted him so bad ah coon't stan' it. Ah hardly had him for a whole day. Ah know foh sure dat man knows sumptin' moh 'bout dat mule."

So the next night he offers four hundred dollars for the mule.

This goes on, back and forth, for a couple of weeks until one night he walks into the bar and slaps a pile of money on the counter. "Ah'll give you *two towsant* dollars foh de mule," he says, "an' dat's mah last deal. Take it oh leave it. Ah'm trew wid selling det mule."

The other man looks at him, and shakes his head. "Ah kin't sell you de mule," he says.

"You kin't sell our mule? What you talkin' 'bout?" the first man says.

"Ah kin't sell de mule."

"Why kin't you sell de mule?"

"Becuz after you walked out of heah last night," the second man says, "a stranger walked in, an' he offa'd me fifteen hunnert dollars foh de mule. So ah done solt him."

The first man loses his head. "Wait a minute! Let me git dis straight!" He says. "Is you tryin' ta tell me dat you went an' sole dat mule ta a complete stranger—whan de two of us bin making a good livin' on dat mule?!!"

Mais, you kin talk about dat pie—or you kin eat it.

Her gumbo's so thin, de moh you ate, de hon-grier you git.

De time ta peel your crawfish is *befoh* you eat dam.

Allays save one piece o' bread foh soppin' up de gravy.

Doan give me no coffee you kin read de news-paper trew.

You kin't just *eat* it, mah boy—you got ta *talk* dat food down.

De moh de ingredients, de better de jambalaya.

That's the truth! And you also have to cut them up in the right-size pieces. If the pieces are too big, there's not enough surface to capture the sauce (that's what we mean by tex-ture*). If the pieces are too small, they* become *sauce.*

She's so noivous, her, she kin hear de rice growin'.

She's as noivous as de cat in a room full of rockers.

Ambition puts de Tabasco in yo' patience.

Tie her hans so she kin't talk.

"Cajun Fare"

VIVRE POUR
MANGER:
LIVE TO EAT

Once you've eaten in South Louisiana, you'll never be bothered further by Benjamin Franklin's saying, "Live to eat; don't eat to live." I remember a smokehouse known as Mieux's (pronounced "Moes") south of Lafayette on the road to Abbeville that specialized in roasting a duck inside a chicken inside a turkey! You won't find the word *cholesterol* in the Cajun dictionary.

On a recent visit to my maternal cousin Hubert Martel's, his wife Viola first served us coffee the old-fashioned way—on a tray, with the spoons in the half-filled cups of dark roast ready for adding cream and sugar. The brand is Community or Seaport, and 100% coffee; it's the New Orleans folks who add chicory to it, not the Cajuns. Coffee is always served to guests immediately upon their arrival. After coffee, comes dinner at ll:30 A.M. This was Tuesday's fare: pork roast, rice, and gravy; *maque choux* (mock-SHOE): fresh corn, prepared Cajun country-style; snap beans; potatoes; and *andouille* (an-DO-we) sausage; roast chicken; sliced cucumbers and tomatoes fresh from the garden; and my favorite butter beans. Dinner is always followed with coffee and *un gateau* (in this case, a moist coconut cake). It's no wonder another cousin, Sullivan "Buddy" Aguillard (known in French as "Bo-DO"), recommends a jigger of olive oil to coat the stomach before a large meal (this also works to prevent hangovers if you're planning to dance through the night at Fred's).

It's not that Cajuns eat every meal as though it were their last, although before they got to Louisiana that might indeed have been the case. Nowadays it's almost the opposite: the first thing everyone starts talking about the moment they sit down to a meal is *any meal but this one*. It's like birds sending signals to each other, through the fog: "Is we still alive?" "Do you tink we kin fly trew dis stuff?" It's also part of Cajun *indirectness*. Instead of complimenting the food directly, you begin dinner (the midday meal) with allusions to legendary meals of the past or future (daring this meal to take its eventual place among them):

"Boy, do ah remember de time we ate dose shrimp on Grand Isle—Co-yai! dat was some good good shrimp!"

"Yah, why doan we git some dem shrimp foh supper?"

"You 'member dat time we at so much *boudin* (boo-DAN) we fell asleep on de floor?"

"Ah 'member we played *bourré* till foh in de mohnin' an' de only one winnin' was *Mémère*."

Meanwhile fingers are flying, peeling the crawfish (*Mémère* used to peel them for me. She'd peel twenty tails for every one of mine, feeling sorry for my being out of the loop way off in Los Angeles instead of practicing my peeling skills and increasing my speed week after week, year after year, as she had been doing all her life). And no, we don't *all* suck on the heads. Some Cajuns don't even eat crawfish; they prefer shrimp.

My personal favorite recipe is my Aunt Martha's steak and gravy.

Doan put all yo' eggs in one pocket, no.

Any kind o' medicine woiks if you wan' it ta woik bad enough.

De skonk's territory ain't negoshable.

You kint he'p bein' who you are, so you bedder make de most of it!

Whan you do good t'ings on purpose, better t'ings start happenin' by theyselves.

LIFE PRESERVERS IN THE SEA OF STORIES

Sometimes folks have stolen wisdom from Louisiana without giving credit. The one that gets me angriest is Churchill saying, "He's lak a man what feeds an alligator hopin' it'll ate him last." I mean, how many alligators do you think there are in England? What adds to these sayings' pungency, for me, is that they serve as life preservers tossed into the sea of stories. Uncle Ed would be in the middle of a two-hour story when suddenly Aunt Willie would throw in a saying that seemed to bring the story, for that instant, to a point: "Doan put all yo' eggs in one pocket, no." The point wakes us up, keeps us on track, makes us nod and laugh—and pay attention so we understand what the story was getting at. My brother Fred will leave the room the moment he hears anyone even *suggest* that I tell the story about the oranges.

De time ta pay de fiddler is *befoh* de dance.

Action is de fiddle ta de feet o' talk.

He kin't dance foh steppin' all ovah his own feet.

Take yo' time hurryin' over dah.

It's hard ta wake a man what ain't sleepin'.

She talks deeper dan she thinks.

Dis menu reads better dan it eats.

Co-yai! was she perty! Everywhar ah'd look she was perty.

Ah keep lookin' at mah han', *sha*, but all ah kin still see is mah fingers.

The old man is listening to the young man telling him that the money "dey bin plannin' to make on de crawfish trap scheme he talkt him into is comin', foh sho'—it's jes' takin' a little longer dan he was hopin'—and when it comes it's gonna be much *more dan dey 'spected an'—" The old man interrupts him with, "Ah tell you sumptin' boy. Ah keep lookin' at mah han' an' all ah kin still see is mah fingers."*

Dat boy's not complicated enough ta unnerstan' hisself.

Tell de trewt—*mais*, yah—but run!

On de day you win you ain' gonta be tired no moh.

De bigger de temptation, de moh guts it takes ta yield ta it.

Doan waste yo' time wid little t'oughts. Scare yo'self big!

You wanta build a big house, yah? Dig a big hole.

Dat woman's lak a shoo-fly—she gits her tongue inta everyting!

He doan say much 'cause he doan have nuttin' ta say.

If ah die ah forgive you—if ah live, we'll see 'bout dat.

If you dream muddy water, dah's bad trouble ahead.

You doan win de big purse from racin' wid an ass.

Him, he been feedin' dat alligator, hopin' it'll ate him last.

AUNT MARTHA'S STEAK AND GRAVY

She uses round steak, which she's seasoned liberally with salt, cayenne, and black pepper. She browns the whole steak in oil in the bottom of her Magnalite until the bottom is crusted. Then she raises the crust with water, in which she's simmered onions, celery, green bell peppers, and sometimes a few hot peppers and garlic (diced).

Now more water and Cajun seasoning is added to the pot and the steak is cut into three-inch squares and simmered until it's well-done (Cajuns don't trust rare meat). When the meat is cooked, flour is added to the liquid for thickening, and a dash of Kitchen Bouquet to deepen the gravy's color and flavor. Always serve with rice, and plenty of bread for sopping the gravy.

I *gorantee* you'll love it.

"**A**t a Crab Boil"

Learnin' begins at de table.

Cut it in little pieces, *sha*, so we kin all have moh.

If you got ta axe foh sumptin' ta eat, you in de wrong kitchen.

Me, ah doan lak ta eat wid a man what shits in his own *courtbouillon*.

Give me a old enemy ovah a new friend *any-time*.

Dere ain't no bosses in de swamp.

Bones don't float.

This is a warning: Back off, or you'll find yourself at the bottom of the bayou.

If a man kin fiddle good enough, he doan need a woman.

A man wid nuttin' ta lose is dangerous, yah.

Stay out o' de middle o' someone else's quick-sand.

Photo by Russell Lee

"Playing the Slot Machines"

Lady luck 'ventually favors de mad.

Yo' kin't shake bad luck—you jes' got ta distract it.

Doan t'ink it's det easy ta ketch de moon in yo' teeth.

Doan git embarrassed till you done messed up good.

If you ain't scairt, you ain't doin' anyting wort'w'ile.

De man what says it kin't be done should not git in de way o' de man doin' it.

She's tryin' ta walk away from her own shadda.

Ah doan have ta talk, me. Mah wife talk so good she says everyt'in.

What's de point o' livin' dis long if yo' gone ta start rememberin' everyting?

Till you know whar ta go foh sure you not goin' nowhar.

No use to worry whar you goin' till you know foh sure whar you at.

It's better ta be attacked dan be ignored.

If you hate yo' parents, boy, keep yo' own rifle out o' de bushes.

This doesn't have a lot to do with rifles. It means, if you can't get along with your Daddy and Momma, you better think twice about ploughing your own field and planting your own seed.

"The Crossroads Store"

POETIC JUSTICE

In the little town of Natchitoches (Nag-i-TOSH), an old man named Mr. Cady used to spend most of his waking hours at the country store, sitting in a steer-hide rocking chair on the front porch, telling tall tales to the kids in the town who had nothing better to do than listen to him all day.

The kids would go home and tell the stories to their dads. Most of them went something like this:

"In mah own tahm," Mr. Cady told them, "we din't have de kind of fancy guns an' ammunition y'all's fathers is used ta. Huntin' used ta be a man's woik, not even a sport—because dey was nuttin' sportin' about it. It was you against de bears, an' all you had—if you was lucky—was a Bowie kinfe, or your bare hands.

Now ah know y'all's dads go huntin' every yeah, but it's too bad in a way because de bears doan have a chance against dem. With automatic rifles an' shotguns, it's a wonder dere is any bears left at all."

It didn't take too long before the young fathers of the village, in danger of losing the affection, loyalty, and respect of their sons, decided it was time to fix Mr. Cady's wagon. They got together one night at the bar and figured it out. The next day, they were at the general store bright and early to invite Mr. Cady to go with them on the annual hunt.

"Oh, no, y'all, ah trewly appree-she-ate de offer, ah do," Mr. Cady says, "but mah time has come an' gont. Ah know y'all doan wan' an old fart lak me along. Ah'm really fine sitting heah by myself, tinking 'bout de old days lak ah do."

They insisted. "Mr. Cady, our boys have tole us what a great hunter you was, what a great tracker, an' we want you ta pass along all dat knowledge ta us."

Mr. Cady starts sweatin' a little because he always knew in his heart that his mouth was going to get him in trouble, and now here come the judge. No matter what he said, the men insisted. "We'll pick you up at tree in de mohnin'. You just bring yo'self some lonch, an' doan worry 'bout anyting else."

"What about mah old squirrel gun?" Mr. Cady asked, just testing the waters.

"Doan worry about dat, neither," they answered. "We know

you doan need a gun, an' dat's why we invitin' you. You jes' come along yo'self."

"Mah knife?"

"Leave your knife at home."

Mr. Cady knew right then and there that his goose was cooked. On the way home that night, he thought back over the last twenty years or so—on all the good feelings he had from telling those stories on the store porch. All the respect and admiration. All the disdain he'd caused among the youngsters of the town toward their newfangled fathers. If he was planning to bargain with his maker, he for sure wasn't going to start denying he deserved what was coming to him.

That night, he tossed and turned, but no matter how little he slept and how much he fretted, the morning came along anyway. There they were, outside the door, in their trucks, waiting for him, with strong coffee in their hands and big laughs on their faces. Old Mrs. Cady just shook her head and sent her husband on his way.

When they reached the camp after driving half the day and hiking into the piney woods till the sun went down, Mr. Cady said, "Lissen. Ah'll tell you what. Y'all know what a good cook ah am. Why doan y'all let me rustle up some cornbread foh y'all in de morning, an' while y'all is checking out de situation ah'll be fixin' y'all some filé gumbo for lunch. Then what ah have in mind for dinner is, depending on how well y'all do, either some bear steaks or a little rabbit pie with fresh baby okras, which ah brought along with me in mah bag."

They laughed and thanked him, and sent him off to bed, saying, "Nossir, Mr. Cady, you're heah ta show us how ta hunt lak men, an' whan we git up in de mohnin', dat's exactly what you're gone ta do. You're gone ta lead us out lookin' foh bear, an' whan you find dem foh us, you gone ta show us how ta deal wid dem bears wid your bare hands."

Mr. Cady started to say something, but bit his tongue. He realized his time was running out, and went on to bed. But it came to him in a dream what to do. The next morning, way before sunup, he crawled out of the cabin and across the stump-dotted clearing and marched into the woods.

"What ah'll do," he figured, "is scout around de area, then come back at sunup an' tell them ah've checked out de situation an' must report dat we wastin' our time heah—no bears *dis* season." He liked the sound of this, and part of him was convinced it would work—even though he suddenly realized he couldn't even *remember* how long it had been since he'd seen a wild bear in the flesh—if indeed he had ever seen one at all.

He was nosing around in the woods, trying to make as little noise as possible, when, as luck would have it, he almost tripped over a young bear cub whose head was half-buried in a blackberry bush. The bear cub turned to yelp at him, and Mr. Cady turned on his heel to head back to the clearing. Turned right into the maw of an outraged she-bear, on her hind legs, claws extended, roaring at the old man who had just threatened her cub's foraging. Mr. Cady's hair, what little he had left of it, stood on end.

The bear didn't give him a lot of time for thinking. Mr. Cady ran for dear life, the bear on his tail, going through all the prayers he could remember. He knew he was paying the price for all those years of stories. He thought it wasn't right to complain about it, but then he thought, de hell wid it, and said to *le bon Dieu*, "Lissen, you let me off de hook dis time, an' ah will *nevair* tell one story again, no matter what, as long as ah live."

Meanwhile he was running as fast as his old legs could carry him through the clearing. He could smell the bear's breath, could hear her breathing on the back of his neck. His imagination was going crazy, thinking about how he was going to taste to that old bear.

Running straight for the door of the cabin, Mr. Cady's vision was blurred with fear, his heart beating so hard that he tumbled head over heels over a stump, then up against the door, which opened into the cabin filled with sleeping men.

The bear hit the stump a split-second after, and went tumbling after Mr. Cady into the cabin. Mr. Cady was already on his feet, to face the terrified waking men.

"Y'all skin dis one!" he shouted. "Ah'm gone back foh some moh!"

You learn moh from yo' losses dan from yo' wins.

Every good kick in de butt moves you 'long.

Yo' kin't win if you doan stay in.

Ah doan let 'im bodar me 'less ah feel lak it.

He's not woith de powder it take ta blow him up!

He'd hand somebody a pipe bomb an' stand dere talkin'.

Dat man's so smart he doan make any sense.

Nuttin' woise den a downhill pat'h det doan lead home.

To de worm in de cow flop, de whole *worl'* is cow flop.

"**A**dvertising for Frogs"

Eatin' is believin'.

You kin't live wid a woman what won' cook garlic.

Ah'd radder have me a poun' o' bacon dan a hill o' dreams.

De best way ta change yo' hosban', *sha*, is ta leave him.

Mais, dere's a woman after mah own mouth.

If yo' not talkin' ta yo'self, you talkin' ta de wrong folks.

Ah tell you one ting—you got ta have a good roof beneath yo' feet.

De moh she apologized de madder she got.

Dat woman's mouth allays trips her up.

She turns up just often 'nuf ta keep herself woiked up.

He's in de right business, yah, jes' in de wrong haid.

We all *born* crazy, *sha*—de hard ting is ta *stay* dat way.

He's not smart nuff ta be dat crazy.

De moh he ate her gumbo, de moh pissed off he got.

Come heah, *sha*, an' put yo' finger in mah coffee.

The Cajun way of saying, "You're sweet!"

It's hard ta kill a Aguillard. Ain't enough ta cut off dey's haid—you got ta bury it!

At de end o' de worl' we *better* be dancin'.

Photo by Russell Lee

"**R**eturning from Early Morning Fishing"

BASIC CAJUN SURVIVAL GLOSSARY

andouilles a hard, smoked, highly seasoned Creole-Acadian pork sausage originating in communities along the lower Mississippi River. Andouilles are served with eggs for breakfast, with rice and andouille gravy for dinner, and as a spicy addition to gumbo, jambalaya, and fresh field vegetables.

bayou a slow-moving, often mossy, often brown, fish-teeming, vegetation-lush body of water. From the Choctaw Indian word for "creek"—but don't try to tell anyone from South Louisiana that a bayou is a creek. When you see the word *creek*, you're in *North* Louisiana or you're not in Louisiana at all.

boudin (boo-DAN) a pork-blood sausage, highly seasoned and containing rice. Try them from Johnson's grocery store in Eunice. They say a Cajun seven-course meal is a six-pack of beer and boudin.

courtbouillon (coor-boo-YON) a spicy and delicate sauce for fish, one of the most refined dishes in the Cajun repertoire.

cracklins (French: gratons) the crisp pork-rind that remains after the skin has been rendered for lard.

Creole Don't try to tell somebody something's Creole unless you're willing to fight to the death for your viewpoint. This is the most hotly debated word in the vocabulary of Louisiana, not to be used loosely, and if you want to hear all about it, call me.

"dirty rice" a Louisiana dish of rice cooked with bits of liver or meat and seasoned with green pepper, etc. Used for stuffing or served by itself.

etouffée (ay-too-FAY) method of cooking, usually shrimp or crawfish, "smothered" in chopped vegetables over low flame. Served over rice.

fais-do-do (fay-doe-DOE) a dance party.

filé (FEE'-lay) thickening powder made from dried sassafras leaves, found on sassafras trees along the Gulf Coast, used as a seasoning for gumbos and jambalayas, usually at the point of serving.

gumbo From the African *gombo* meaning "okra." The French bouillabaisse evolved into a rich, hearty, roux-based soup, served over rice, that can no longer be recognized as its predecessor. There are many varieties today as there are families in Louisiana.

jambalaya highly seasoned Creole-Cajun dish including several meats and fish as well as rice. Not to be confused with gumbo.

"the King Fish" Governor Huey Long, who transformed the face of Louisiana with modern highways and bridges until he was assassinated in the state capital in Baton Rouge.

lagniappe (la-NYAP) "something extra"—a Cajun custom. Always throw in a little *lagniappe*, whether it's at the bakery (with an extra cookie added to the dozen), in the gumbo pot, or an extra "tip."

maque choux (mock-SHOE) a corn dish (best with spring shoe-peg corn), served with bits of tomato, green bell pepper, onion, and lots of pepper.

Mardi Gras "Fat Tuesday," the last day of feasting and celebration before the Lenten season of fasting and celebration begins. In other places this is known as "Carnival." The most authentic surviving celebration is the "run Mardi Gras" in Mamou (pronounced mom-MOO).

parish "county" in other states, but Louisiana still operates under Napoleonic Code, not U.S./British Common Law, and the parish is the seat of local administration. Famous Cajun parishes include Evangeline, St. Landry, Acadia, Calcasieu.

pirogue (PEE-rogue) small, flat-bottomed Cajun boat invented for use in the bayous, usually propelled by poles.

roux (roo) a smooth mixture of lard or butter and flour, heated over low flame slowly until it turns a nutty brown. A thickening agent for soups, bisques, sauces, and gravy.

T- abbreviation of the diminutive "*petit*" (small), also sometimes spelled "ti" as in Ti-Jean ("little John," because he is anything but little).

Tabasco the hottest of pepper sauces, from peppers grown and bottled in New Iberia, Louisiana. They say a relationship isn't serious until a couple is on their second bottle of Tabasco.

tasso (TASS-oh) a highly spiced, lean smoked meat, similar to jerky. Used as a flavoring, but also eaten as is.

About de author

Kenneth Aguillard Atchity, president of Atchity Entertainment/Editorial International in Los Angeles, is a literary manager and independent producer, author of books (including *A Writer's Time: A Guide to the Creative Process, from Vision through Revision* and *The Mercury Transition: Career Change Empowerment Through Entrepreneurship*) and screenplays (including, with Alexander Viespi, *Dead South*, set in Napoleonville, Louisiana). He is de son of Myrza Aguillard of Eunice, Louisiana, grandson of Mezille Latiolais of Henderson and Evan Aguillard of Eunice. He took hisself a wrong turn at Cocodrie, passed through Carencro, ended up at Georgetown and Yale, and, as a result, has to have his Community coffee, crawfish, and cracklins shipped ta him in de mail.

If you have Cajun lore or photos you'd like to share, the author would love to hear it:

Kenneth Atchity
AEI
9601 Wilshire Blvd. #1202
Beverly Hills, CA 90210
FAX 213-932-0321